12-99

SCIENCE ESSENTIALS CHEMISTRY

Acids and Alkalis

DENISE WALKER

EVANS
LONDON

© Evans Brothers Ltd 2007

Published by:
Evans Brothers
2a Portman Mansions
Chiltern Street
London W1U 6NR

Series editor:
Harriet Brown

Editor:
Harriet Brown

Design:
Simon Morse

Illustrations:
Ian Thompson, Simon Morse

Printed in China by
WKT Company Limited

British Library Cataloguing in
Publication Data

 Walker, Denise
  Acids and alkalis. - (Science
  essentials. Chemistry)
  1. Acids - Juvenile literature 2.
  Alkalis - Juvenile
  literature
  I. Title
  546.2'4

 ISBN-10: 0-237-53002-3

 ISBN-13: 978-0-237-53002-0

Contents

Introduction

Acids and alkalis are found in a surprising number of places. Some acids and alkalis are edible and are found in foods. Others are very strong and can be harmful, such as the acid in car batteries and the alkali in oven cleaners.

This book takes you on a journey to discover more about acids and alkalis. Find out what they are, how they affect other substances and why we need them. Discover how acid rain forms and how it affects the environment, learn about indicators and make your own indicator out of cabbage leaves. You can also find out how acids and alkalis are used in fire extinguishers, discover how neutralisation reactions work and see how you can use this knowledge to stop bee and wasp stings from hurting.

This book also contains feature boxes that will help you to unravel more about the mysteries of acids and alkalis. Test yourself on what you have learnt so far; investigate some of the concepts discussed; find out more key facts; and discover some of the scientific findings of the past and how these might be utilised in the future.

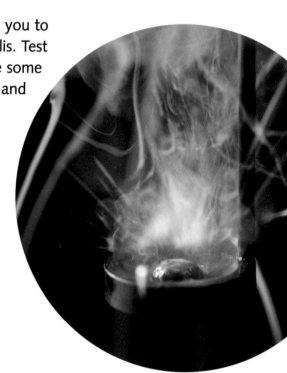

Acids and alkalis are all around us. When you have read this book, you too will understand how important acids and alkalis are to our lives.

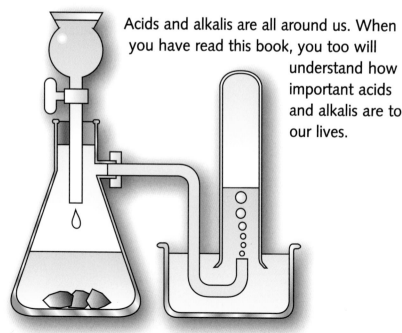

DID YOU KNOW?

▶ Watch out for these boxes – they contain surprising and fascinating facts about acids and alkalis in the world around us.

TEST YOURSELF

▶ Use these boxes to see how much you've learnt. Try to answer the questions without looking at the book, but take a look if you are really stuck.

INVESTIGATE

▶ These boxes contain experiments that you can carry out at home. The equipment you will need is usually cheap and easy to find around the home.

TIME TRAVEL

▶ These boxes describe scientific discoveries from the past and fascinating developments that pave the way for the advance of science in the future.

ANSWERS
At the end of this book on pages 46 and 47, you will find the answers to the questions from the 'Test yourself' and 'Investigate' boxes.

GLOSSARY
Words highlighted in **bold** are described in detail in the glossary on pages 46 and 47.

1

What are acids and alkalis?

We often associate the term 'acid' with a dangerous substance that can cause us harm. Most concentrated acids are dangerous and very **corrosive** and must be handled with care. The same is true of concentrated **alkalis**. But acids and alkalis are not always dangerous. For example, lemon juice and vinegar are acidic, and bicarbonate of soda, which is used in cake baking, is alkaline.

WHAT IS AN ACID?

An acid is defined as 'a substance that **dissolves** in water and forms hydrogen **ions** (H^+)'. We can also describe an acid as a substance that dissolves in water and forms protons. A hydrogen atom only contains one proton in its nucleus and has one electron circling the nucleus. When the hydrogen atom loses its electron to form a hydrogen ion, this leaves behind just one proton. Therefore, a hydrogen ion is sometimes called a proton.

▲ The warning triangle on the right means that the substance involved is an irritant. The one on the left means that the substance is corrosive.

HYDROGEN ATOM   **HYDROGEN ION**

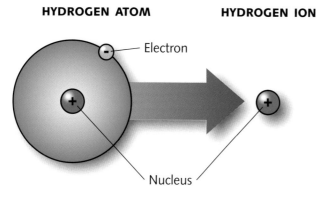

Electron

Nucleus

PROPERTIES OF ACIDS

▶ Acids can be corrosives or **irritants**. When acids are concentrated, they can burn bare skin. You must take care and wear gloves when using these acids. Less concentrated acids are not as harmful and are described as 'irritants'. These acids cause an itching sensation if spilled on bare skin.

▶ All acids have a sour taste. Some acids are present in foods that we use for flavouring. Vinegar contains ethanoic acid. Lemons and other citrus fruits contain citric acid. Vinegar and citrus fruits have a sharp taste which we describe as 'sour'. All acids have a sour taste, but you MUST NOT test this for yourself.

▶ All acids must be dissolved in water in order for hydrogen ions to form.

▶ All acids will change the colour of another chemical substance called an **indicator**. The presence of an acid can be detected by adding an indicator.

Useful acids

▶ The proteins that make up our bodies are made from smaller units called amino acids.

▶ Vitamin C is another name for ascorbic acid. This is needed by our bodies to keep healthy. Vitamin C can prevent a disease called scurvy.

▶ Salicylic acid is used to make aspirin.

▶ The acid found in car batteries is called sulphuric acid. This is a very corrosive acid, which is why car batteries must be handled with care.

▶ The food that we eat is digested in our stomachs in the presence of hydrochloric acid. This is also a very corrosive acid which explains why our stomachs are lined heavily with tissue that is not easily corroded.

▶ One of the most corrosive acids is called hydrofluoric acid. This acid is so corrosive that it will chemically attack a glass bottle if stored in this way. Hydrofluoric acid must be stored in a plastic container. This property of hydrofluoric acid is utilised in glass etching.

▲ Citrus fruits contain ascorbic acid. This is not a strong acid and it will not damage your mouth when you eat it.

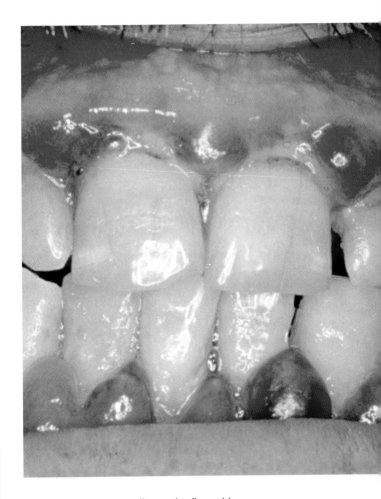

▲ These gums are swollen and inflamed because the patient has a vitamin C (ascorbic acid) deficiency and has developed scurvy.

INVESTIGATE

▶ **You must ask an adult for permission before carrying out the following experiments.**

Experiment 1
Take a chicken bone and immerse it in vinegar overnight. What happens to the bone?

Experiment 2
You will need a fresh egg, a bottle with a neck that is slightly smaller than the egg and some vinegar. Soak the egg in the vinegar for approximately two days. Carefully squeeze the egg into the bottle. Does it go all the way in? How does this work?

ACID RAIN

Vehicles burn fuel and emit a gas called sulphur dioxide (SO_2) into the atmosphere. Sulphur dioxide is a colourless gas that has a choking smell. Sulphur dioxide is the main cause of **acid rain**, although nitrogen oxides (also from the burning of fuels) also contribute to acid rain. Sulphur dioxide gas rises into the atmosphere and dissolves in rain clouds to form a weakly acidic solution. A series of chemical reactions produces sulphuric acid (H_2SO_4) in rain clouds – acid rain.

WHAT HAPPENS WHEN ACID RAIN FALLS TO THE EARTH?

When the acid rain falls to the Earth it can:

▶ **Damage buildings made from sedimentary rock.**

When acid reacts with calcium carbonate (limestone), the rock becomes worn away. The chemical equation for this reaction is:

Calcium carbonate + Sulphuric acid ⟶ Calcium sulphate + Water + Carbon dioxide

$$CaCO_{3(s)} + H_2SO_{4(aq)} \longrightarrow CaSO_{4(aq)} + H_2O_{(l)} + CO_{2(g)}$$

▶ **Make ponds and lakes more acidic.**

Many living organisms are sensitive to these changes and cannot easily survive in acidic conditions.

▶ **Strip away tree bark, which can kill the tree.**

Whole forests can be destroyed if acid rain falls in large enough quantities.

▶ **Damage metallic constructions.**

Acid rain chemically attacks metal and produces a salt and hydrogen gas. The chemical equation for this reaction is:

Iron + Sulphuric acid ⟶ Iron sulphate + Hydrogen

$$Fe_{(s)} + H_2SO_{4(aq)} \longrightarrow FeSO_{4(aq)} + H_{2(g)}$$

▶ This forest in Poland has been destroyed by acid rain. It is likely that the sulphur dioxide and nitrogen oxides were released by vehicles and factories thousands of miles from the forest. The gases would have been carried in the atmosphere by the wind until they fell as acid rain.

WHAT ARE BASES AND ALKALIS?

Bases are compounds that can neutralise acids. When they react in appropriate proportions, a neutral product is achieved. The product of a **neutralisation** reaction is called a **salt**. Bases are usually metal oxides, metal hydroxides, metal carbonates or metal hydrogencarbonates. Ammonia is also a base and has the formula NH_3.

Many bases are insoluble in water. When a base is soluble in water, it is called an alkali. When a base dissolves in water to form an alkali, it releases hydroxide ions (OH^-). In summary:
▶ An alkali is a base that is soluble in water.
▶ All alkalis are bases.
▶ Only soluble bases are alkalis.

PROPERTIES AND USES OF BASES AND ALKALIS

Some bases and alkalis can be corrosive at high concentrations. They must be treated as carefully as acids. Bases have a bitter, rather than a sour taste, but you MUST NOT taste them. Bases and alkalis can feel soapy to the touch, although it is also dangerous to do this because they can burn the skin.

Bases and alkalis are used to neutralise acids. They are often used in cleaning products. Alkalis and bases are important for certain chemical reactions.

For example, some fire extinguishers contain acids and hydrogencarbonates. When the two chemicals react together, carbon dioxide gas is produced. As the pressure of the carbon dioxide builds up, it is expelled from the extinguisher at high speed to smother a fire.

▼ This electrical fire is being put out with carbon dioxide which can be produced by reacting an acid and a base.

2

Measuring acidity and alkalinity

How do we know if a substance is an acid or an alkali? For safety reasons, we cannot taste or feel the substance, so we must use chemical testing. One of the simplest methods of determining whether a substance is acidic or alkaline is to use an indicator. An indicator is a substance that will change colour in the presence of an acid or an alkali.

LITMUS

Litmus is one of the most commonly used indicators. It is available in two colours – blue litmus and red litmus. It can be used as a paper or in solution. When you add an acid to litmus, the indicator turns (or remains) red. When you add an alkali, the indicator turns back to (or remains) blue. Litmus is extracted from plants called lichens, which grow on rocks and trees. Scientists have used litmus indicators for over 400 years.

Adding an acid or an alkali to litmus produces a chemical change that can only be reversed by adding the opposing substance. If you have added an acid, you can restore the original colour by adding an alkali. You cannot simply remove the original acid.

Use the following to help you to remember the colour changes of red and blue litmus:
AciDs turn litmus reD. ALkalis turn litmus bLue.

Red litmus	Blue litmus
Red in acid	Red in acid
Blue in alkali	Blue in alkali

▶ These orange and white lichens are growing on a rock. Lichens are used to make litmus indicator.

OTHER INDICATORS

Natural indicators are extracted from plants, but chemists have also developed many other chemical indicators. The following table shows some common indicators and the colour changes they show in acids and alkalis. Notice that their chemical names give no indication of their origins, but it is worth remembering that many come from plants.

Indicator	Colour in acid	Colour in alkali
Methyl orange	Red	Yellow
Methyl red	Red	Yellow
Phenolphthalein	Colourless	Pink

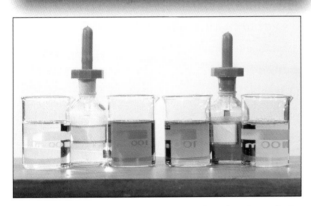

▲ Phenolphthalein is colourless in acid and pink in alkali (left). Methyl orange is red in acid and yellow in alkali (right).

DID YOU KNOW?

▶ Gardeners need to know whether their soil is acidic or alkaline. Some plants flourish in one condition whilst different plants flourish in the other. Gardeners can buy kits that help them to determine how acidic their soil is, but there are some flowering plants that will provide this information naturally. Hydrangeas are flowering shrubs. In acidic soil, the flowers are blue and in more alkaline soil the flowers are pink. It is also possible that flowers from one shrub begin pink, but after soil treatment, turn blue!

▶ **The acidity of the soil affects how easily the hydrangea can take up aluminium. This is what changes the colour of the flower.**

INVESTIGATE

▶ **Ask an adult's permission before trying the following experiment.**

The aim of this experiment is to make an indicator from common kitchen and garden ingredients, and test it using some kitchen acids and alkalis.
To obtain the indicator, use the following steps:
(1) Chop some red cabbage and boil it in a saucepan of water until the colour of the water does not change any further (it will be purple).
(2) Put a colander over another large pan, and pour the cabbage into the colander. Keep the coloured water.
(3) Discard the cabbage.
(4) Allow the water to cool.

You must wear a laboratory coat, rubber gloves and goggles for the next part of the experiment.

To use the indicator, follow these steps:
(1) Ask an adult to help you to pour some household ammonia or oven cleaner into a glass.
(2) Pour some lemon juice into a second glass.
(3) Add a small amount of your prepared indicator (cabbage water) to each of the liquids.
(4) Observe the colour changes.
Which colour shows that the substance is an alkali and which colour shows that the substance is an acid?

STRONG AND WEAK ACIDS AND ALKALIS

Chemists describe an acid as being either strong or weak. All acids contain hydrogen. When acids break down, they release hydrogen ions. Substances that do this successfully are strong acids and those that do not easily release hydrogen ions are called weak acids.

The strength of an acid is not related to how concentrated or dilute it is but rather is related to its ability to break down and release hydrogen ions. For example, the acid in vinegar is ethanoic acid. This is a weak acid – no matter how much acid is present, or how concentrated it is, the acid will not easily release hydrogen ions. It will not cause any damage if spilt on human skin.

▼ This beaker contains a very strong acid – hydrochloric acid. It is a volatile liquid (**evaporates** easily) which is why you can see vapours rising from the surface.

The same principle is applied to an alkali. Alkalis contain hydroxide ions and strong alkalis break down to release many of these ions. Weak alkalis will not break down as readily.

THE pH SCALE

A definite measure of acidity or alkalinity is carried out using the pH scale. pH stands for 'power of hydrogen'. The scale runs from pH 1 to pH 14. A neutral substance has a pH value of 7. Numbers lower than pH 7 indicate an acid, with pH 1 indicating a strong acid, such as hydrochloric acid. Very weak acids have pH values of around 5 or 6. Acid rain is a weak acid.

A value higher than pH 7 indicates that the substance is alkaline. Strong alkalis, such as sodium hydroxide, have pH values of between 12 and 14. Values between pH 8 and 9 indicate very weak alkalis. Seawater is a weak alkali.

pH SCALE

pH values	Examples
pH = 1	Battery acid
pH = 2	Sulphuric acid
pH = 3	Vinegar
pH = 4	Orange juice
	Acid rain (4.2-4.4)
	Acidic lake (4.5)
pH = 5	Bananas (5.0-5.5)
	Clean rain (5.6)
pH = 6	Healthy lake (6.5)
	Milk (6.5-6.8)
pH = 7	Pure water
pH = 8	Seawater
pH = 9	Baking soda
pH = 10	Milk of magnesia
pH = 11	Ammonia
pH = 12	Caustic soda
pH = 13	Bleach
pH = 14	Liquid drain cleaner

MEASURING pH

The simple indicators that we have met so far, change colour at specific pH values. Not all indicators change colour at the same pH, however. One very useful indicator, which changes colour over the entire range of pH values, is **universal indicator**. This substance is a mixture of several different indicators, all of which have specific colour changes at particular pH values. In acidic substances, universal indicator displays a range of colours from red to yellow. In alkaline substances, universal indicator can be any colour from green to dark purple.

Universal indicator is available as a solution or in paper form. Solution works best if you have a colourless substance to test, such as seawater. You can add drops of the solution to the substance and observe the colour change. To use paper, place a strip of the paper on a substance, for example a bar of soap. The paper changes colour. It is best to use paper if you have a dark-coloured substance to test. If you used indicator solution in a dark liquid, you would not see the colour change.

UNIVERSAL INDICATOR

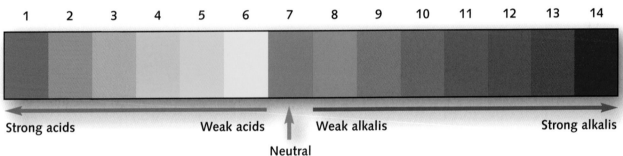

USING TECHNOLOGY TO MEASURE pH

pH can also be measured using a pH probe. The probe consists of a glass bulb that contains a thin strip of platinum wire. Platinum is used because it remains chemically unaffected by any hydrogen ions in the test solution. Before the probe is dipped into the test solution, it is calibrated using a solution of known pH value. This is called a **buffer solution**. By doing this, you make sure that the probe is measuring pH accurately.

When the probe is dipped into an acidic or alkaline test solution, hydrogen ions move into the glass bulb. The probe converts this into a pH value which is read from the display on the probe. Some pH probes are linked to computers and the values are logged over time.

TEST YOURSELF

▶ What colour would you expect the following solutions to turn in the presence of universal indicator? What pH value would this indicate?

(1) Vinegar

(2) Ammonia solution

(3) Pure water

Neutralisation reactions

Substances that do not change the colour of simple indicators, or that turn universal indicator green, are described as neutral. Neutral substances have a pH value of 7. Table salt and a solution of sugar and water are neutral substances. Neutral substances can also be produced through neutralisation reactions. These reactions occur between an acid and an alkali.

HOW DO NEUTRALISATION REACTIONS WORK?

When an alkali is slowly added to an acid, the hydrogen ions in the acid react with the hydroxide ions in the alkali until they are all eventually used up. At this point there are no solitary hydrogen or hydroxide ions present and water is produced. The chemical equation for this reaction is:

Hydrogen ions + Hydroxide ions $\longrightarrow$ Water

$H^+ + OH^- \longrightarrow H_2O$

Any other ions from the acid and alkali combine together to form a type of compound called a salt.

WHAT IS A SALT?

In chemistry, a salt is a compound that is made up from a metal component and a non-metal component. Salts are ionic compounds. They contain positively charged ions and negatively charged ions. The charges cancel each other out and the salt has no overall charge.

SODIUM CHLORIDE STRUCTURE

EXAMPLES OF NEUTRALISATION REACTIONS

(1) SODIUM HYDROXIDE AND HYDROCHLORIC ACID

Sodium hydroxide and hydrochloric acid react together as follows:

Sodium hydroxide + Hydrochloric acid $\longrightarrow$ Sodium chloride + Water

$NaOH_{(aq)} + HCl_{(aq)} \longrightarrow NaCl_{(aq)} + H_2O_{(l)}$

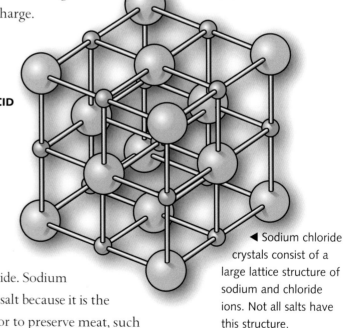

◀ Sodium chloride crystals consist of a large lattice structure of sodium and chloride ions. Not all salts have this structure.

This produces water and a salt called sodium chloride. Sodium chloride is sometimes called common salt or table salt because it is the substance that we put on our food to add flavour, or to preserve meat, such as salted beef. However, the sodium chloride that we eat has usually been mined or obtained from salt water, rather than being created through this type of reaction.

(2) POTASSIUM HYDROXIDE AND SULPHURIC ACID

Potassium hydroxide and sulphuric acid will also react together in a neutralisation reaction as given by the equation below:

Potassium hydroxide + Sulphuric acid $\longrightarrow$ Potassium sulphate + Water

$$2KOH_{(aq)} + H_2SO_{4(aq)} \longrightarrow K_2SO_{4(aq)} + 2H_2O_{(l)}$$

Potassium sulphate is a salt, but this is not one that we would sprinkle on our food!

USES FOR NEUTRALISATION REACTIONS AND SALTS

Salts and neutralisation reactions are very useful and have a range of applications in everyday life.

▶ Neutralisation has an application in agriculture. When farmers grow fields of crops, the growing plants remove important nutrients from the soil. This can make the soil acidic and unsuitable for further plant growth. Lime is sprayed onto the soil to neutralise the acidity. Lime is also called calcium oxide and is a base.

▶ People suffering from indigestion take tablets called antacids. Indigestion is a condition in which there is too much acid in the stomach. Antacids contain magnesium hydroxide or aluminium oxide which react with stomach (hydrochloric) acid in the following way:

Magnesium hydroxide + Hydrochloric acid $\longrightarrow$
Magnesium chloride + Water

$$Mg(OH)_{2(aq)} + 2HCl_{(aq)} \longrightarrow MgCl_{2(aq)} + 2H_2O_{(l)}$$

Magnesium chloride is a salt that can pass safely through the body.

DID YOU KNOW?

▶ Bee stings are acidic. Treatments that relieve the pain are alkaline. They work by neutralising the acid from the sting. Some soaps are alkaline and can relieve bee sting pain.

▶ Wasp stings are alkaline. They are neutralised by applying acidic substances, such as vinegar.

▶ If you are stung by a nettle, you will get a painful rash. Nettles give you a dose of methanoic acid. Nettle stings can be alleviated with dock leaves, a weed that often grows near nettles. Dock leaves contain a neutralising base which relieves the symptoms of the sting.

▲ After a bee stings someone, it tries to fly away. The stinger rips from the bee, causing the bee to die.

TITRATION

Titration is a very accurate laboratory technique used to find the exact point at which neutralisation occurs. This point is sometimes called the **end point**. There are two parts to titration – making a **standard solution** and carrying out a neutralisation reaction.

(1) MAKING A STANDARD SOLUTION

A standard solution is a solution of known concentration. Chemists use a **volumetric flask** (sometimes called a graduated flask) to make a standard solution. Volumetric flasks come in a variety of sizes, and each one measures only one volume of solvent. For example, a 250 millilitre volumetric flask cannot be used to measure 100 millilitres of solvent. Volumetric flasks have only one marking on them.

The table below shows the steps used to make a standard solution of an acid:

VOLUMETRIC FLASK

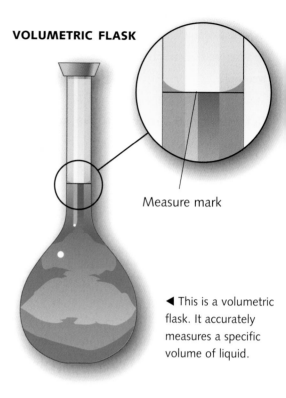

Measure mark

◄ This is a volumetric flask. It accurately measures a specific volume of liquid.

Step	Procedure	Explanation
1	Weigh the solid acid in a **weighing boat**.	The weighing scales are accurate to two or three decimal places and can record the mass accurately.
2	Transfer the solid to a beaker and rinse the weighing boat with distilled water. Put the distilled water from the boat into the beaker. When dry, re-weigh the boat.	All of the weighed solid has been transferred to the beaker and this is checked by re-weighing the boat.
3	Add a little distilled water to the beaker. Use a glass rod to crush and dissolve the solid.	The solid is dissolved before it is transferred to the volumetric flask. It is not easy to dissolve a substance in a volumetric flask because of its shape.
4	Once dissolved, pour the solution through a filter funnel into the volumetric flask. Rinse the beaker, funnel and glass rod with distilled water and add this to the volumetric flask.	All material has been added to the flask and all apparatus is carefully rinsed to make sure no acid solution has been left behind.
5	Add distilled water until the flask is full up to the line.	When the water level sits just on the line then the flask has been used correctly and exactly the correct amount of solvent has been added.
6	Shake the solution before you remove a sample.	Each time the solution is used, it must be shaken thoroughly. This action ensures thorough mixing.

(2) CARRYING OUT A NEUTRALISATION REACTION

A **pipette** and a **burette** are used in this part of the technique. A pipette accurately measures just one volume of solution and is used to add the standard solution to a conical flask. A burette accurately measures different volumes of solution and is used to slowly add the alkali (or acid) to the standard solution.

The table below shows the steps for a neutralisation reaction:

▼ This student is filling a pipette with a standard solution of acid that he will put into the conical flask. The burette on the left is filled with an alkali.

Step	Procedure	Explanation
1	Add a set amount of the standard solution to a conical flask, using a pipette.	The conical flask is used because its shape is ideal for swirling and mixing the solution.
2	Add two or three drops of an indicator to the contents of the conical flask.	The indicator makes the point of neutralisation easier to detect because it will change colour when neutralisation is reached.
3	Fill a burette with the solution of unknown concentration. This can be either an acid or an alkali (in our example it is an alkali).	The burette must not contain any air bubbles, and an initial reading is taken. This is the level at which the acid or alkali sits at the beginning of the experiment.
4	Add the solution from the burette slowly until the indicator just changes colour. Constantly swirl the conical flask. Take a reading from the burette.	The flask is swirled to ensure thorough mixing. When the indicator just changes colour, another reading is taken from the burette so the chemist knows exactly how much solution has been added.
5	Repeat the procedure, but much more slowly, until consistent readings are obtained.	The first reaction was a trial and gives a rough guide to the point of neutralisation. When repeated, the procedure can be slowed down so that the exact point of neutralisation can be obtained.

▶ This student is adding an alkali to a standard solution. The standard solution contains indicator. When it changes colour, the point of neutralisation has been reached.

MEASURING pH IN A TITRATION

The best indicators change colour at a particular pH, rather than gradually over a series of pH values.

(1) A STRONG ACID AND A STRONG ALKALI

Phenolphthalein, methyl orange and methyl red are suitable indicators for the titration of a strong acid and a strong alkali. When the alkali is slowly added to the acid, and the pH is measured using a pH probe, chemists can plot a graph (top right).

(2) A WEAK ACID AND A STRONG ALKALI

Phenolphthalein is a suitable indicator for this titration. The graph begins at a higher pH because a weak acid is being used. The point of neutralisation is still quite sharp, nevertheless, and the remainder of the graph looks much like the first graph.

(3) A STRONG ACID AND A WEAK ALKALI

Methyl red and methyl orange are suitable indicators for this titration. The starting point of this titration is the same as in the first example because a strong acid is being used. However, because we are using a weak alkali, the point of neutralisation is much higher on the vertical part of the graph and the final part of the line is flat.

(4) A WEAK ACID AND A WEAK ALKALI

In reality this type of titration is rarely carried out because it is almost impossible to locate the exact point of neutralisation. The change in pH on the line graph is very gradual. The pH of the initial acid and the alkali are both close to 7. The point of neutralisation at pH 7 is in the middle of the line on the graph.

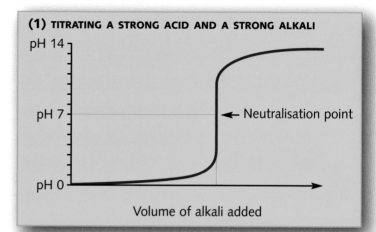

(1) TITRATING A STRONG ACID AND A STRONG ALKALI

pH 14 / pH 7 / pH 0 — Neutralisation point — Volume of alkali added

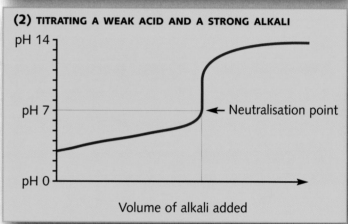

(2) TITRATING A WEAK ACID AND A STRONG ALKALI

pH 14 / pH 7 / pH 0 — Neutralisation point — Volume of alkali added

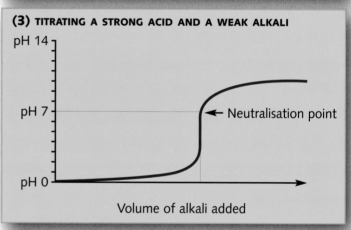

(3) TITRATING A STRONG ACID AND A WEAK ALKALI

pH 14 / pH 7 / pH 0 — Neutralisation point — Volume of alkali added

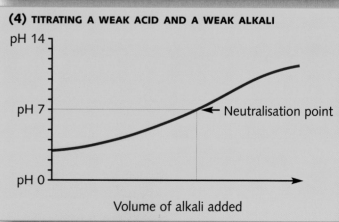

(4) TITRATING A WEAK ACID AND A WEAK ALKALI

pH 14 / pH 7 / pH 0 — Neutralisation point — Volume of alkali added

Salts, solutions and solubility

In chemistry, a solution is a mixture of one or more solutes dissolved in a solvent. The solute is often a solid and the solvent is almost always a liquid. For example, when you add sugar to a cup of tea, the sugar is the solute and the tea is the solvent. Together they make a solution.

Solute + Solvent ⟶ Solution

Some salts are soluble, which means that they will dissolve in a solvent. Other salts are insoluble. Knowledge of the solubility of salts helps chemists to identify them.

SOLVENTS

Water is known as a universal solvent, which means that it is freely available and can dissolve many substances. There are plenty of other solvents, too. Nail varnish remover is a solvent. It dissolves nail varnish and removes the varnish from the fingernails. Alcohol is an important solvent for products such as perfume and aftershave. It dissolves the scent, and when sprayed onto skin, the solvent quickly evaporates and leaves the scent behind.

SOLUBILITY

Solubility is a measure of how soluble a solute is in a solvent. Have you ever tried to dissolve sugar into cold water or milk? You may have noticed how if you sprinkle sugar onto your cereal, there is often some left at the bottom of the bowl. However, if you dissolve sugar into a hot liquid, with just a little stirring, it will dissolve quite easily. This shows that substances dissolve better in hot solvents than in cold solvents. The complete opposite is true if the solute is a gas.

Solubility is usually temperature dependent. Solubility is measured by the number of

grammes of solute that will dissolve in 100 grammes of solvent at a particular temperature. There is no pattern to the solubility of different solutes and it is not easy to predict. The following graph shows the solubility of two common salts.

SOLUBILITY OF TWO SALTS WITH TEMPERATURE

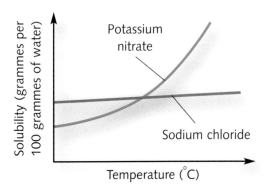

SATURATED SOLUTIONS

Saturated solutions are solutions into which no more solute will dissolve at a certain temperature. For example, at room temperature, 30 grammes of sodium chloride will easily dissolve into 100 millilitres (100 grammes) of water. If an extra 10 grammes of sodium chloride is now added, 4 grammes remains undissolved because the solution has become saturated. The solubility of sodium chloride is therefore 36 grammes of solute in 100 grammes of water at 20°C.

SUMMARY

▶ 30 g sodium chloride + 100 g water =
130 g solution

▶ 130 g solution + 10 g sodium chloride =
140 g in the container

▶ But 4 g of the 40 g sodium chloride added remains
undissolved and $40 - 4 = 36$

▶ In total, 36 g of sodium chloride will dissolve
in 100 g of water.

SOLUBILITY RULES

If a substance can dissolve in water, it is soluble and
will dissolve up to a certain concentration. Once a
solution becomes saturated, however, the substance
is no longer soluble. If a substance is described as
insoluble this means that the majority of it will not
dissolve into solution. When an insoluble substance
is put into a solvent, it forms a **suspension**. A
suspension is a solid substance that floats in a solvent.

The solubility of salts follows particular rules:

Type of salt	Soluble	Insoluble
Chlorides	Most are soluble	Silver chloride and lead chloride
Sulphates	Most are soluble	Barium, calcium and lead sulphates
Nitrates	All are soluble	None are insoluble
Carbonates	Sodium and potassium carbonates	Most are insoluble
Ethanoates	All are soluble	None are insoluble
Sodium, potassium and ammonium salts	All are soluble	None are insoluble

▲ These stalactites and stalagmites are made of
calcium carbonate, which is insoluble in water.
Calcium carbonate reacts with rainwater and
forms soluble calcium bicarbonate. When the
water drips from cave ceilings, calcium carbonate
precipitates from the water droplets and creates
these incredible natural structures.

TIME TRAVEL: CARBON SINKS

Carbon dioxide is an acidic gas. This means that it dissolves in water to form a weakly acidic solution called carbonic acid. This is a very important process because it helps to kerb climate change. Carbon dioxide is a greenhouse gas and when it builds up in the atmosphere it contributes to global warming. Approximately two-thirds of the Earth is covered in water and a lot of the carbon dioxide that is produced through everyday human activities dissolves in the oceans. This is called the carbon sink.

Throughout history, massive amounts of carbon dioxide released by animals and other natural processes have been absorbed into the carbon sink, and the amount of carbon dioxide in the atmosphere has remained steady for the last 650,000 years. However, since the development of electricity, cars and factories, carbon dioxide emissions have significantly increased.

During the 1980s and 1990s, about half of all carbon dioxide emissions remained in the atmosphere, 20 per cent was taken up by plants through photosynthesis and a huge 30 per cent went into the oceans.

Today, the amount of carbonic acid in the oceans has increased dramatically, changing the chemical composition of the water. The increased acidity has a direct effect on organisms such as coral whose bodies are made of carbonates. A chemical reaction occurs between the seawater and the carbonates in the coral. The coral breaks up and disappears. This is yet another reason why it is so important to reduce carbon emissions.

▼ When excess carbon dioxide is dissolved in the oceans, the seawater becomes more acidic. This can harm marine organisms.

MAKING PREDICTIONS ABOUT SOLUBILITY

A number of rules can be used to make predictions about the outcome of reacting two substances together. For example, the reaction between silver nitrate and sodium chloride produces silver chloride and sodium nitrate. The equation for this reaction is:

Silver nitrate + Sodium chloride $\longrightarrow$ Silver chloride + Sodium nitrate

$AgNO_3 + NaCl \longrightarrow AgCl + NaNO_3$

Using the rules from our solubility table on page 20, we know that silver nitrate, sodium chloride and sodium nitrate are soluble. They would be in an aqueous solution. Silver chloride is insoluble and so would appear as a precipitate (a solid substance formed when two or more solutions react together). The state symbols for this reaction can now be inserted into the equation:

$AgNO_{3(aq)} + NaCl_{(aq)} \longrightarrow AgCl_{(s)} + NaNO_{3(aq)}$

SEPARATING SOLUTIONS

There are a wide range of chemical techniques that allow us to separate solutions.

EVAPORATION

When you gently heat a solution, the liquid part evaporates from the surface until only the solid is left behind. Notice how a dish with a large surface area is used for evaporation. This is called an evaporating dish. It is placed over a water bath because if you heat the solution directly until no liquid is left, some of the solid material can decompose and the solution can 'spit' dangerously. It is best to evaporate most of the solution over the hot water bath, and leave the rest to evaporate naturally in a sunny window.

▲ This copper sulphate solution is being evaporated over a water bath.

CRYSTALLISATION

This technique is similar to evaporation. You heat a solution so that the solvent begins to evaporate. This concentrates the amount of solute in the solution. Continue to heat the solution until you have a saturated solution. Remove it from the heat and leave it to cool. Crystals of solute will begin to appear.

CHROMATOGRAPHY

In this technique, you place a spot of solution on a surface such as absorbent filter paper. Place one end of the paper into a beaker of solvent. The solvent should travel slowly up the paper and carry the solution with it. Remove and dry the paper and you will notice small spots of solute. The solute has been successfully separated from its solution and you can scrape it off the paper.

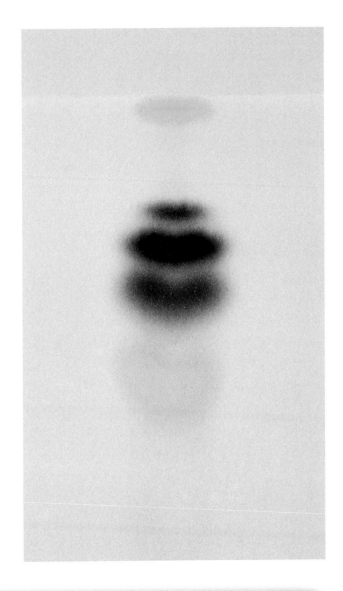

▶ This is a chromatogram of an extract from meadow grass. The different coloured bands represent different chemicals. The orange band (top) is carotene, the green bands are different chlorophylls, and the yellow (bottom) represents other carotenes.

TIME TRAVEL: INTO THE FUTURE

Scientists are trying to find out why the tumours of some cancer patients grow faster than others. They hope that a greater understanding of tumours may reduce cancer deaths in the future. Chemistry is coming to the rescue. Fried foods contain linoleic and linolenic acids. Research has shown that the proportions of these two acids in food can affect how quickly cancerous tumours grow. For example, in one study when cancer patients ate food that contained these acids in a ratio of 9:1 or higher, their tumours grew more quickly.

A team of students at a school in Kansas, USA, tested chips in a selection of local restaurants.

Their experiment involved (1) extracting oil from the chips using a solvent, (2) separating the particles in the oil using a centrifuge (a rapidly spinning machine), (3) evaporating the solvent, and (4) reacting another solvent with the fatty acids to find out the ratios of linoleic to linolenic acids.

They found that some chips contained linoleic and linolenic acids at an incredibly high ratio of 17:1. Some chips had a much lower ratio of 3:1 and these chips had a double layer of batter on them. Now the race is on to find out whether the low ratio chips are actually healthier for us and if so whether it really is the batter that makes them healthier.

USEFUL SALTS

Salts have been used by people for many years. Here, we will explore some of the uses for salts in the past, present and the future.

LIVER SALTS

Liver salts are taken by people who suffer from acid indigestion. Liver salts contain sodium hydrogencarbonate (which is also called sodium bicarbonate). This is an alkali. The stomach naturally produces hydrochloric acid to help digest food. However, if someone eats a particularly rich or large meal, the stomach may produce excess acid. Unfortunately, this can cause a lot of discomfort. The alkaline liver salts react with the hydrochloric acid in the following way:

Sodium hydrogencarbonate + Hydrochloric acid $\longrightarrow$ Sodium chloride + Carbon dioxide + Water

$$NaHCO_{3(aq)} + HCl_{(aq)} \longrightarrow NaCl_{(aq)} + CO_{2(g)} + H_2O_{(l)}$$

The sodium hydrogencarbonate neutralises the acid. You may feel like 'burping' afterwards because of the build-up of carbon dioxide gas.

GLAUBER'S SALT

The common name for this salt is sodium sulphate and it is a **hydrated salt**. This means that water molecules lie amongst its salt structure. It was discovered by Johann Glauber in the 1600s and was originally used as a laxative. Today, the main use for Glauber's salt is as an ingredient in powdered laundry detergents.

Other uses for sodium sulphate are:

▶ To prevent the formation of small air bubbles in molten glass.

▲ When sodium hydrogencarbonate reacts with acid, it releases bubbles of carbon dioxide.

▶ To help dyes stick to materials during textile manufacture.

▶ As a heat storage component in solar heating systems. This is still being researched for use in the future.

Approximately half of the world's supply of Glauber's salts is found naturally, particularly in lakes in Canada. The other half is produced artificially – some is produced as a by-product of other important chemical reactions. For example, both the production of hydrochloric and sulphuric acids results in the formation of sodium sulphate.

Sodium chloride + Sulphuric acid $\longrightarrow$ Sodium sulphate + Hydrogen chloride

$$2NaCl_{(s)} + H_2SO_{4(aq)} \longrightarrow Na_2SO_{4(aq)} + 2HCl_{(g)}$$

GYPSUM

Gypsum's chemical name is calcium sulphate and its formula is $CaSO_4.2H_2O$. Gypsum is used in blackboard chalk and cement. One of its main uses is in drywalls. In 2005, drywalls were the most common material used across the world for the construction of interior walls and ceilings. They are made by forming gypsum into flat sheets, which are then sandwiched between two pieces of heavy paper. Gypsum is a hydrated compound. When it is exposed to heat, such as in a house fire, the water in its structure is converted to steam. The gypsum cannot get any hotter or burn until this water has completely boiled away. Drywalls are therefore fire resistant.

Gypsum occurs naturally and can also be produced artificially. When fossil fuels are burnt, the sulphur inside them is released as sulphur dioxide. This gas is passed through special chimneys called scrubbers where the sulphur dioxide reacts with limestone. This 'cleans' the gas and produces calcium sulphate as a by-product. The gypsum produced by this method is very pure. Gypsum can also be produced as a by-product of phosphate fertiliser refinement.

▲ Glauber's salt (sodium sulphate) is found naturally on lake beds in Canada.

▶ The inside walls of this house are drywalls, which are made from gypsum.

5

Making salts

The five main ways to make salts are:
(1) to react a metal and an acid,
(2) to react an insoluble base and an
acid, (3) to react an alkali and an
acid, (4) to react a carbonate and an
acid, and (5) a precipitation reaction
between two salts.

MAKING SALTS USING METALS

Acids react with most metals and the
reactions always produce salts. These
reactions also produce hydrogen gas.
The general equation for this reaction is:

Metal + Acid $\longrightarrow$ Salt + Hydrogen

This reaction can be very vigorous if a
highly reactive metal, such as sodium,
is used.

POTASSIUM

Potassium is a very reactive metal and
will cause a violent reaction with acids
such as hydrochloric and sulphuric acid.
It is also very reactive with water, which
is described by chemists as an extremely
weak acid.

Potassium + Hydrochloric acid $\longrightarrow$
Potassium chloride + Hydrogen
$$2K_{(s)} + 2HCl_{(aq)} \longrightarrow 2KCl_{(aq)} + H_{2(g)}$$

ZINC

Zinc is not as reactive as potassium. When
you mix a less reactive metal with an acid,
a salt and hydrogen gas are still produced,
but the reaction will be gentler.

▲ This is what happens
when water is dripped onto
potassium metal. This
reaction produces a lot of
heat, potassium hydroxide
and hydrogen gas.

Zinc + Hydrochloric acid $\longrightarrow$

Zinc chloride + Hydrogen

$$Zn_{(s)} + 2HCl_{(aq)} \longrightarrow ZnCl_{2(aq)} + H_{2(g)}$$

TIN

Other metals that are low in the reactivity series will only produce a salt over a long period of time. They may not appear to react at all. For example, tin will occasionally produce a bubble of hydrogen gas when reacted with acid.

Tin + Hydrochloric acid $\longrightarrow$

Tin chloride + Hydrogen

$$Sn_{(s)} + 2HCl_{(aq)} \longrightarrow SnCl_{2(aq)} + H_{2(g)}$$

▲ Zinc reacts with hydrochloric acid and produces zinc chloride and bubbles of hydrogen gas.

TEST YOURSELF

▶ Write balanced chemical equations for each of the following chemical changes:

(1) Calcium and sulphuric acid

(2) Copper and dilute nitric acid

(3) Magnesium and hydrochloric acid

WHICH ACIDS MAKE WHICH SALTS?

It is possible to produce a wide range of salts by varying not only the type of metal, but also the type of acid used in a reaction. The table below summarises the salts that are formed with different acids.

Type of acid	Type of salt produced
Hydrochloric acid	Chloride
Sulphuric acid	Sulphate
Nitric acid	Nitrate
Phosphoric acid	Phosphate

OBTAINING SOLID SALT CRYSTALS FROM SOLUTION

Each of the salts in the above table are soluble and can be found in the mixture of unreacted acid and water. To obtain pure salt crystals, the following steps should be followed:

(1) You must make sure the reaction is fully complete. To do this, add metal to the reaction mixture until you do not see any more bubbles of hydrogen gas.

(2) Heat the solution in a water bath until crystals begin to form.

(3) Leave the solution in an evaporating dish in a sunny window until the crystals of salt fully appear.

INVESTIGATE

▶ Leave an iron nail in an acid solution, such as water mixed with vinegar, lemon juice or cola. Observe the nail after a few days. What has happened to it?

MAKING SALTS USING INSOLUBLE BASES

A salt can be made from the reaction between an acid and an insoluble base. This reaction also produces water. The general equation for this reaction is:

Acid + Insoluble base ⟶ Salt + Water

Oxides are usually insoluble with the exception of ammonium oxide and the group one oxides (sodium oxide, potassium oxide and lithium oxide). Zinc oxide, copper oxide and magnesium oxide are insoluble bases.

The table below summarises the salts that can be made from two common insoluble bases:

Acid	Insoluble base	Soluble salt
Sulphuric acid	Iron oxide	Iron sulphate
Nitric acid	Zinc oxide	Zinc nitrate

COPPER OXIDE + HYDROCHLORIC ACID
Copper oxide is an insoluble base. It will react with hydrochloric acid in the following way.

Copper oxide + Hydrochloric acid ⟶ Copper chloride + Water

$$CuO_{(s)} + 2HCl_{(aq)} \longrightarrow CuCl_{2(aq)} + H_2O_{(l)}$$

HOW TO CARRY OUT THE REACTION
The following procedure is used to react an acid and an insoluble base to produce a soluble salt.

(1) Add a known amount of hydrochloric acid to a boiling tube and warm it. The rise in temperature causes the reaction to proceed at a faster pace.

◀ Warm the acid over a Bunsen burner.

(2) Add solid copper oxide to the warmed acid, one spatula full at a time. Continue to do this until the copper oxide will no longer 'disappear' into the solution. As you add the copper oxide, the reaction proceeds and the solution begins to turn greenish-blue as copper chloride forms. An excess of copper oxide is added to ensure that all the hydrochloric acid has reacted.

(3) **Filter** the excess copper oxide from the solution, which now contains copper chloride and water.

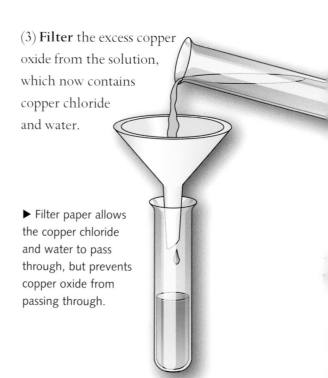

▶ Filter paper allows the copper chloride and water to pass through, but prevents copper oxide from passing through.

(4) Put the copper chloride solution into an evaporating dish and heat it indirectly above a large beaker of water. This limits the spitting that may occur and preserves the quality of the final crystals.

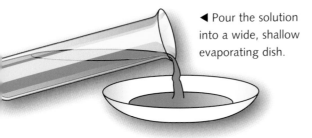

◄ Pour the solution into a wide, shallow evaporating dish.

▼ Place the evaporating dish on a water bath, and heat it over a Bunsen burner.

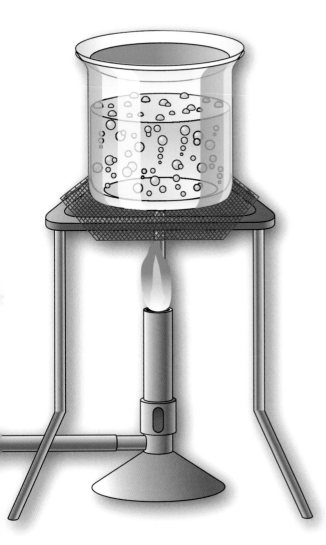

(5) When the first crystals begin to appear, remove the evaporating dish from the beaker and place in a sunny window. The crystals will appear naturally as the water slowly evaporates. The slow evaporation causes the final crystals to be quite large. If you continued to heat the evaporating dish over a water bath, the crystals would form more rapidly but would be much smaller.

▲ Crystals of copper chloride will form gradually as the remaining water evaporates.

SUMMARY

The stages involved in making a salt from an acid and an insoluble base can be summarised by the following terms:

▶ Mixing
▶ Filtration
▶ Evaporation
▶ Crystallisation

TEST YOURSELF

▶ How would you make pure crystals of magnesium sulphate from an insoluble base and an acid? Give the names of the reactants you would use and provide the practical details.

▶ Why would you not use the answer from the question above as a method to make a pure sample of potassium sulphate crystals?

MAKING SALTS USING ALKALIS

A soluble salt can be made from the reaction between an acid and an alkali. Alkalis are soluble bases and usually contain hydroxide ions. Ammonia solution is also an alkali. The general equation for this reaction is:

Acid + Alkali ⟶ Salt + Water

SODIUM HYDROXIDE + HYDROCHLORIC ACID

Sodium chloride can be made by reacting sodium metal and chlorine gas, but this reaction is extremely vigorous and dangerous. A safer way to produce sodium chloride crystals is to react an acid with an alkali.

Sodium hydroxide + Hydrochloric acid ⟶ Sodium chloride + Water

In this case, all the reactants and the final salt are soluble. Retrieving the final product therefore requires some clever laboratory methods.

HOW TO CARRY OUT THE REACTION

The following steps are used in the laboratory to react sodium hydroxide with hydrochloric acid.

(1) Firstly, measure 25 millilitres of sodium hydroxide into a conical flask.

(2) Add three or four drops of phenolphthalein indicator. This indicator is pink in alkaline solutions. (It is important to use a known amount of sodium hydroxide because the experiment will be repeated later without the indicator.)

(3) Fill a burette with hydrochloric acid. Record the volume of acid at the start of the experiment.

(4) Add the hydrochloric acid slowly to the sodium hydroxide in the conical flask. At the same time, gently swirl the conical flask to mix the acid and alkali.

(5) The indicator will turn colourless when all of the alkali has been neutralised by the acid. At this point, do not add any more acid.

▼ This conical flask contains sodium hydroxide and phenolphthalein (which is pink in alkaline solutions). Hydrochloric acid will be added from the burette.

(6) Take a final reading from the burette. To calculate the exact amount of acid added, subtract the second reading from the first. The purpose of this part of the procedure is to measure how much acid is needed to neutralise the initial volume of alkali.

(7) Now repeat the whole experiment but without the use of an indicator. The indicator is not necessary because you have already discovered the amount of acid that is required for neutralisation. The addition of indicator would make the final product impure.

(8) The solution remaining in the conical flask contains sodium chloride and water. Put this in an evaporating dish and heat it indirectly above a beaker of water.

(9) When the first crystals appear, place the evaporating dish in a sunny window. The crystals will slowly form.

TEST YOURSELF

▶ Explain how you would make pure crystals of potassium chloride using potassium hydroxide and hydrochloric acid. State the method that you would use.

DID YOU KNOW?

▶ Forensic scientists use phenolphthalein to test for the presence of blood at a crime scene. They wipe a cotton bud over the suspected sample of blood. Next they add a few drops of alcohol, followed by a few drops of phenolphthalein indicator. Lastly, they add a few drops of hydrogen peroxide.

If the sample on the cotton bud turns pink, then blood is present. Once a scientist has confirmed the presence of blood, they can find out the blood type and analyse the DNA. They may be able to match this information to a person.

The formation of the blood drop on the ground at the crime scene can also tell the scientist whether the person was standing still or moving, and in which direction they were moving.

▶ This forensic scientist is cutting a sample of material from blood-stained jeans. He will analyse the DNA and try to link a suspect with the victim and the crime scene.

MAKING SALTS USING CARBONATES

Another method of making a salt is the reaction between a metal carbonate and an acid. Most metal carbonates are insoluble and the general equation for this reaction is:

Metal carbonate$_{(s)}$ + Acid$_{(aq)}$ $\longrightarrow$
Metal salt$_{(aq)}$ + Carbon dioxide$_{(g)}$ + Water$_{(l)}$

Once all of the metal carbonate has been used up, the soluble salt will be present in the remaining solution. However, as with the previous examples, to ensure that all of the acid has been used up, it is important to use an excess of metal carbonate. This is achieved by adding so much solid that bubbling, and hence the reaction, finishes when there is still some solid carbonate left in the solution.

MAGNESIUM CARBONATE + SULPHURIC ACID

Magnesium carbonate will react with sulphuric acid in the following way:

Magnesium carbonate + Sulphuric acid $\longrightarrow$
Magnesium sulphate + Carbon dioxide + Water
$MgCO_{3(s)}$ + $H_2SO_{4(aq)}$ $\longrightarrow$ $MgSO_{4(aq)}$ + $CO_{2(g)}$ + $H_2O_{(l)}$

HOW TO CARRY OUT THE REACTION

(1) Add a known volume of acid to a test tube.

(2) Spoon the solid metal carbonate into the acid, one spatula at a time. Do this until bubbles are no longer produced and no more metal carbonate will appear to dissolve.

▶ This photograph shows magnesium carbonate reacting with acid, as in step two of the experiment. The reaction is still proceeding because you can see carbon dioxide bubbles forming.

(3) Filter the mixture to remove unreacted metal carbonate from the salt solution. No unreacted acid should now remain in the solution.

(4) Place the salt solution in an evaporating dish on a water bath and heat it.

(5) When crystals begin to appear, the evaporating dish contains a saturated solution. Leave the apparatus in a sunny window until you have crystals of magnesium sulphate.

WEATHERING

Calcium carbonate (limestone) buildings can be corroded by acid rain, which is a dilute solution of sulphuric acid. This produces calcium sulphate, carbon dioxide and water. Limestone is particularly at risk because it is very porous. This means that the rain easily soaks into the rock's tiny pores and attacks it. Notice how the salt produced by this reaction, calcium sulphate, is insoluble and so the rock does not simply disintegrate. However, the two other products, water and carbon dioxide, do leave the rock. The water evaporates and the carbon dioxide passes into the atmosphere. The rock is gradually worn away. The Statue of Liberty in New York, USA, had to be restored because of the damage caused by acid rain. The statue is made from copper. Rain has reacted with the copper, which is why it looks green.

▶ Rain is a weak acid. It attacks buildings that are made from limestone, such as the Louisiana State Capitol building in the USA, and thousands of other buildings around the world.

TEST YOURSELF

▶ Marble is also made from calcium carbonate. It does not become weathered like limestone. Use the internet or the library to find out why differences between marble and limestone mean that marble is not easily weathered.

INVESTIGATE

▶ **Ask an adult before trying this experiment.**

You will need citric acid crystals (available from a pharmacy), bicarbonate of soda and icing sugar. Mix the ingredients together in equal proportions and then put a small amount of the mixture into your mouth. What happens? Use library books or the internet to help you work out the word equation for this chemical change.

MAKING SALTS USING PRECIPITATION REACTIONS

The last method by which salts can be made is through precipitation. This method is chosen when you want to produce an insoluble salt. A precipitate is a solid that is produced as the result of two or more solutions reacting together. This method of making salts is sometimes called **double decomposition**. A general equation for the reaction is:

Soluble salt 1 + Soluble salt 2 $\longrightarrow$ Insoluble salt + Soluble salt 3

LEAD NITRATE + SODIUM SULPHATE

Lead sulphate is insoluble and can be made from the soluble salts lead nitrate and sodium sulphate. The equation for this reaction is:

Lead nitrate + Sodium sulphate $\longrightarrow$ Lead sulphate + Sodium nitrate

$$Pb(NO_3)_{2(aq)} + Na_2SO_{4(aq)} \longrightarrow PbSO_{4(s)} + 2NaNO_{3(aq)}$$

From this example it is easier to see where the name 'double decomposition' comes from – both metal ions switch partners.

HOW TO CARRY OUT DOUBLE DECOMPOSITION

Making an insoluble salt in the laboratory is straightforward. The following steps are used to obtain a pure and dry sample of the salt.

(1) Mix the two soluble salts together in equal proportions. This produces an insoluble precipitate.

(2) Filter the insoluble precipitate from the remaining mixture of solutions. Keep the solid residue because it contains the salt. Dispose of the filtrate (liquid).

(3) If the precipitate has a very thick consistency it may need to be filtered using vacuum pressure. This can be done with a Buchner funnel and Buchner flask. The apparatus is attached to a water tap which is then turned on at full force. The water rushing through the apparatus creates pressure that is sufficient to pull liquid through the filter funnel and into the flask – like a vacuum cleaner's suction. This equipment can be left running to allow the residue to dry further.

(4) The residue on the filter paper is the insoluble salt. Flatten the paper and leave it to dry completely in a dust-free environment.

BUCHNER FILTRATION

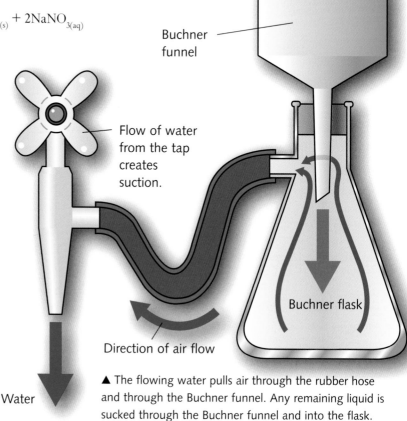

Buchner funnel

Flow of water from the tap creates suction.

Buchner flask

Direction of air flow

Water

▲ The flowing water pulls air through the rubber hose and through the Buchner funnel. Any remaining liquid is sucked through the Buchner funnel and into the flask.

MAKING PAINT

Precipitation reactions are used to produce coloured **pigments** which can be used for paints. The table below shows the colours of different insoluble precipitates:

Name of precipitate	Colour of precipitate
Lead carbonate	White
Lead chromate	Yellow
Iron (III) hexacyanoferrate(II)	Blue
Copper carbonate	Green

▼ This bright yellow precipitate is lead chromate. It has been formed by dripping potassium chromate into lead (ll) nitrate solution.

INVESTIGATE

▶ **Ask an adult before trying this experiment.**

In the 1500s and 1600s, Mughal artists in India made their paints from natural materials, such as stones and minerals, which they ground into fine powders. After grinding, the material was washed to remove impurities. The insoluble material produced was called a pigment and it was mixed with a binding agent. The main binding agent was gum from acacia trees. To allow the pigment to flow better and stick to the cloth, the artists added honey to it.

Use the internet to research Mughal techniques, then try and copy their methods to make your own paint out of turmeric or saffron (ask an adult's permission first because saffron is expensive). You may also be able to extract pigments from kitchen ingredients such as red cabbage or blackberries.

▲ This Mughal painting was painted in 1633.

DID YOU KNOW?

▶ Stink bombs contain a solution of ammonium sulphide ($(NH_4)_2S$). When you crush them, the solution diffuses into the air creating a horrible choking smell. Chemistry can be used to deactivate a stink bomb. If the bomb is opened while it is submerged in a solution of lead nitrate, the following chemical reaction occurs:

Ammonium sulphide + Lead nitrate ⟶ Lead sulphide + Ammonium nitrate

Lead sulphide is a brown, insoluble precipitate. And most importantly, it has no smell!

6

Uses and manufacture of acids

Acids are extremely important to industry and have been in use for hundreds of years. Hydrochloric acid is used to make PVC plastic and numerous pharmaceutical products. Sulphuric acid is used to make fertilisers and detergents. Nitric acid is used to make explosives and rocket fuel. But before acids can be put to use, they must be manufactured.

HYDROCHLORIC ACID

Hydrochloric acid (HCl) is a solution of hydrogen chloride gas dissolved in water. Hydrogen chloride is a white and very soluble gas, which dissolves readily in water. Hydrochloric acid is a strong acid. It gives away its H^+ ions easily.

USES OF HYDROCHLORIC ACID

▶ Manufacture of other chemicals

The main use of hydrochloric acid is for the production of other chemicals, such as calcium chloride (used in road salt), nickel chloride (used for electroplating) and zinc chloride (used in batteries).

▶ Water softening

Ion exchange resins are used to soften water, which is important in the treatment of drinking water. Hydrochloric acid is used in the manufacture of ion exchangers. The exchangers swap the ions that make the water hard for other ions. For example, calcium and sodium ions are responsible for making water hard. When the water passes through an ion exchanger, these ions are removed.

▶ Control of pH

Hydrochloric acid is used to regulate pH conditions. For example, the food and pharmaceutical industries require a carefully controlled water pH. Hydrochloric acid is used to achieve this. It is also used to maintain the pH of swimming pools.

▶ Steel pickling

The acid removes rust from iron or steel before the metal is made into cans or wires.

◀ A mixture of salt and grit is deposited onto the road surface from the back of this snow-clearing machine. Calcium chloride is the most effective salt to use for melting ice and snow. It also prevents the ice and snow from bonding with the road surface.

Time travel: Hydrochloric acid

Hydrochloric acid was first discovered in 800 CE by Jabir Ibn Hayyan. He was born in Iran but spent much of his life in Iraq and Yemen. He is also credited with the discovery of many other chemicals including citric acid, nitric acid and acetic acid.

Alchemists (early chemists) used hydrochloric acid in their search for 'the philosopher's stone', which was believed to bring the secret of eternal life. Alchemists made hydrochloric acid by reacting sodium chloride with sulphuric acid. The equation for this reaction is:

Sodium chloride + Sulphuric acid $\longrightarrow$
Sodium sulphate + Hydrogen chloride
$$2NaCl_{(s)} + H_2SO_{4(aq)} \longrightarrow Na_2SO_{4(aq)} + 2HCl_{(g)}$$

Next, the hydrogen chloride would have been dissolved in water. This must be done very carefully because of the gas' extreme solubility.

▼ **Jabir Ibn Hayyan, sometimes referred to as the Father of Chemistry, is shown here teaching at a school in Mesopotamia (now Turkey).**

During the Industrial Revolution in the UK in the 1800s, demand for alkaline substances such as soda ash (sodium carbonate) and sodium and potassium hydroxides increased, and large scale production of these materials was developed. One of the by-products of the processes was hydrogen chloride gas and until 1863, this was released directly into the air. In 1863, the 'Alkali Act' was passed in Parliament which obliged manufacturers to dissolve the waste gas into water, to reduce air pollution. This produced hydrochloric acid on a large scale.

In the 1890s, production of industrial alkalis was replaced by the Solvay process. This did not produce hydrochloric acid as a by-product and so other means of producing the acid were sought. In 1926, hydrochloric acid became important in the manufacture of PVC (poly vinyl chloride). This plastic has changed our world. Today, approximately 20 million tonnes of hydrogen chloride gas is produced annually and is made into hydrochloric acid.

HOW IS HYDROCHLORIC ACID PRODUCED TODAY?

▶ As the by-product of the production of chlorine and an alkaline salt, such as sodium hydroxide. In this process, electricity is passed through sodium chloride solution. This produces three substances – hydrogen, chlorine and sodium hydroxide. When the hydrogen and chlorine are allowed to recombine, hydrogen chloride gas is produced.

$$Cl_{2(g)} + H_{2(g)} \longrightarrow 2HCl_{(g)}$$

The hydrogen chloride gas is dissolved in water to produce hydrochloric acid.

▶ By the reaction between sulphuric acid and sodium chloride.

▶ As part of the production of **organic compounds**.

Organic compounds include Teflon (see 'Did you know?' box, below left), PVC, and CFCs. CFCs were used in refrigerators and aerosols until scientists discovered that they harmed the Earth's ozone layer.

SULPHURIC ACID

Sulphuric acid (H_2SO_4) was discovered around 1,200 years ago by alchemists and has been a useful chemical ever since.

THE CHEMISTRY OF SULPHURIC ACID

Sulphuric acid has some unique properties. It can be used to extract water from many chemicals. This makes it useful as a drying agent – it can remove moisture from air and from compounds such as sugar and starch. Sulphuric acid is also an **oxidising agent**. In this reaction it can dissolve some metals and form sulphur dioxide gas.

DID YOU KNOW?

▶ Phosgene (COCl₂) is a chemical weapon that was used in the First World War. When phosgene dissolves deep into the lungs, it forms hydrochloric acid. This acid damages the lining of the lungs and makes them fill with fluid. A similar process occurs with mustard gas. When it dissolves into moist areas such as lungs or eyes, hydrochloric acid forms, causing irreversible tissue damage.

▶ In 1938, an accident led to the discovery of Teflon. The scientists involved believed that they could make a new refrigerant by mixing a compound called TFE with hydrochloric acid. They filled canisters with TFE and froze them. The next day they opened the canisters and tried to pour the TFE into vessels of hydrochloric acid. The first canister gave nothing out, and felt heavier than was expected. The canister was cut open and inside was a waxy white solid – a chemical reaction had taken place. This new chemical was a good lubricant and was chemically unreactive – it also had a very high melting temperature. The solid became known as Teflon and is now used for the surfaces of non-stick pans.

▲ Sulphuric acid poured into a beaker of sugar causes this drying reaction. The black pillar is dried sugar – carbon.

USES FOR SULPHURIC ACID

▶ Approximately 60 per cent of all sulphuric acid manufactured is used to make phosphoric acid. Phosphoric acid is very important for the production of fertilisers and detergents. Another fertiliser, ammonium sulphate, is also made using sulphuric acid.

Ammonia + Sulphuric acid ⟶ Ammonium sulphate

▶ Sulphuric acid is used to make paint, soaps, dyes, plastics and soapless detergents such as shower gel. It is also used in the manufacture of toilet paper.

▶ Sulphuric acid is used in the manufacture of aluminium sulphate which is important in the paper-making process. Aluminium sulphate is produced by the reaction between sulphuric acid and aluminium oxide.

▲ Sulphuric acid is involved in the manufacture of paints.

Use of sulphuric acid	Percentage of acid
Fertilisers	30
Paints and pigments	14
Detergents and soaps	13
Plastics	13
Dyes	2
Steel making	1
Other	27

SELF-CLEANING GLASS

One of the more interesting uses for sulphuric acid is in the manufacture of 'self-cleaning' glass. This glass can break down a grease layer of up to 200 nanometres every single day!

The glass is covered with a clear film of titanium dioxide. This top layer is a **catalyst**. It speeds up chemical reactions in the presence of the Sun's energy. When sunlight shines onto the titanium dioxide, the energy from the Sun makes the layer very reactive. As dirt and grease fall on the layer, a chemical reaction takes place. The products are usually carbon dioxide and water, which run off the windows leaving them perfectly clean.

▲ In the future, self-cleaning glass could be used for high-rise buildings. At the moment, people must scale these buildings to clean the glass.

Manufacture of sulphuric acid
– THE CONTACT PROCESS

In the contact process, sulphur dioxide is turned into sulphur trioxide which is then dissolved in water to produce sulphuric acid. The following steps describe the contact process.

(1) The production of sulphur dioxide.
Firstly, sulphur is burned in air.

Sulphur + Oxygen $\longrightarrow$ Sulphur dioxide

$$S_{(l)} + O_{2(g)} \longrightarrow SO_{2(g)}$$

Notice that liquid sulphur is used. This is sprayed into a furnace.

(2) The production of sulphur trioxide.
Next, sulphur dioxide is mixed with air and passed through a catalyst called vanadium oxide. The catalyst causes the reaction to proceed at a faster rate. The mixture is heated to 450°C and sulphur trioxide is produced.

Sulphur dioxide + Oxygen $\longrightarrow$ Sulphur trioxide

$$2SO_{2(g)} + O_{2(g)} \longrightarrow 2SO_{3(g)}$$

(3) The production of a very concentrated form of sulphuric acid called oleum.
The sulphur trioxide is passed through an absorber, which contains some sulphuric acid. Sulphur trioxide dissolves in the acid and produces oleum.

Sulphur trioxide + Sulphuric acid $\longrightarrow$ Oleum

$$SO_{3(g)} + H_2SO_{4(aq)} \longrightarrow H_2S_2O_{7(l)}$$

(4) Production of sulphuric acid.
The final stage is to carefully dissolve oleum in water to produce sulphuric acid (H_2SO_4).

Oleum + Water $\longrightarrow$ Sulphuric acid

$$H_2S_2O_{7(l)} + H_2O_{(l)} \longrightarrow 2H_2SO_{4(aq)}$$

Notice that when very high concentrated solutions are produced, the state symbol 'l' is used instead of 'aq' because very little water is present. Many of the reactions involved in the contact process release heat – they are exothermic reactions. This heat is not wasted. Instead, the heat is used to make steam which is then used to power parts of the factory. This helps to cover the cost of running the factory.

▲ This massive chemical factory in Germany produces oleum and sulphuric acid.

NITRIC ACID

Jabir Ibn Hayyan (see page 37) is credited with discovering nitric acid, in 800 CE.

USES FOR NITRIC ACID

▶ Nitric acid is used in the manufacture of the explosives nitroglycerine and trinitrotoluene, which were both developed in the middle of the 1800s. They are used to blast rocks apart in mining and quarrying.

▶ Nitric acid is also used in the manufacture of the fertilisers ammonium nitrate and sodium nitrate. These fertilisers are produced by neutralisation reactions. This equation shows the reaction that produces ammonium nitrate:

Ammonia + Nitric acid ⟶ Ammonium nitrate

$$NH_{3(aq)} + HNO_{3(aq)} \longrightarrow NH_4NO_{3(aq)}$$

▶ Drug manufacture and the manufacture of synthetic fibres, such as nylon, require nitric acid. Nylon was first developed as a substitute for silk, which is produced by silk worms. Today, nylon is used to make toothbrush bristles, clothing, ropes and carpets.

▶ A more unusual use for nitric acid is to combine it with hydrochloric acid to make aqua regia. This solution is one of the few that is capable of dissolving gold and platinum.

▼ This close-up photograph of velcro shows a woven base with hooks coming from it. A loop is caught on the hook. This links the two surfaces of the velcro together. Velcro is made of nylon. Nitric acid is used to manufacture nylon.

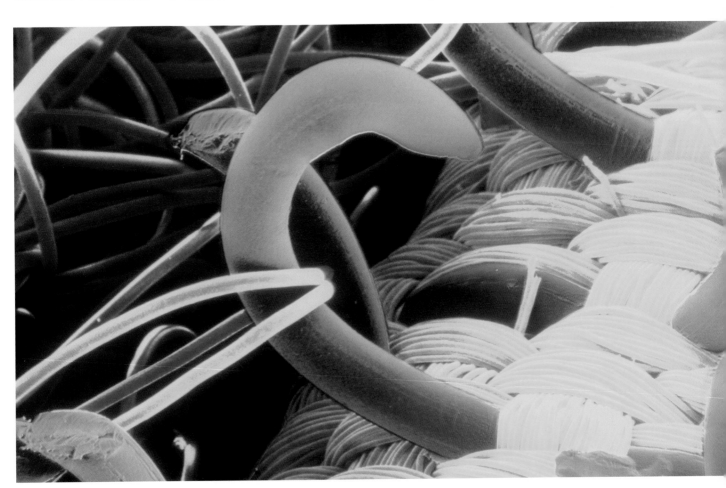

MANUFACTURE OF NITRIC ACID
— THE OSTWALD PROCESS

Nitric acid is produced in the Ostwald process. The most important ingredient in this process is ammonia, which comes from the Haber process. The Haber process converts hydrogen and nitrogen into ammonia in the following reaction.

Hydrogen + Nitrogen $\longrightarrow$ Ammonia

$$3H_{2(g)} + N_{2(g)} \longrightarrow 2NH_{3(g)}$$

Most of the ammonia from this process is converted into fertilisers, but a small proportion is saved for nitric acid manufacture. The following steps describe the Ostwald process (nitric acid manufacture).

(1) Production of nitrogen monoxide.

Ammonia is mixed with air and passed over a catalyst made from a mixture of platinum and rhodium. The mixture is heated to 900°C. This reaction produces nitrogen monoxide and water.

Ammonia + Oxygen $\longrightarrow$ Nitrogen monoxide + Water

$$4NH_{3(g)} + 5O_{2(g)} \longrightarrow 4NO_{(g)} + 6H_2O_{(g)}$$

(2) Production of nitrogen dioxide.

The mixture of nitrogen monoxide and water is cooled and allowed to react with more oxygen.

Nitrogen monoxide + Oxygen $\longrightarrow$ Nitrogen dioxide

$$2NO_{(g)} + O_{2(g)} \longrightarrow 2NO_{2(g)}$$

(3) Production of nitric acid.

Even more air is added and the nitrogen dioxide is mixed with water. This produces nitric acid.

Nitrogen dioxide + Oxygen + Water $\longrightarrow$ Nitric acid

$$4NO_{2(g)} + O_{2(g)} + 2H_2O_{(l)} \longrightarrow 4HNO_{3(aq)}$$

Companies that manufacture nitric acid must be extra careful to ensure that no nitrogen dioxide or nitrogen monoxide escapes from the factory. This is because the gases will dissolve in rain clouds and become one of the ingredients that causes acid rain. Also, it is essential that no nitric acid goes down the drain. It would find its way into rivers and lakes and destroy the wildlife that lives there.

◀ These workers are installing platinum-rhodium sheets, which act as catalysts in the first stage of nitric acid production.

DID YOU KNOW?

▶ In 1845, a German chemist, Christian Schönbein, was experimenting in his kitchen when he spilled a mixture of nitric acid and sulphuric acid. To clean the spillage he used a cotton apron, which he then hung on the stove to dry. A little while later once the apron had dried, it exploded in a flash – he had invented an explosive called nitrocellulose, or guncotton. The nitric acid and the cellulose had caused the following reaction:

Nitric acid + Cellulose ⟶ Nitrocellulose + Water

$$2HNO_3 + C_6H_{10}O_5 \longrightarrow C_6H_8(NO_2)_2O_5 + 2H_2O$$

The nitrocellulose contains fuel and oxygen within one chemical, which is what makes it explode.

▶ In 1867, Alfred Nobel, a Swedish scientist, invented dynamite. Nitroglycerine is the basis of dynamite and is made by mixing glycerol, sulphuric acid and nitric acid. Alfred Nobel developed nitroglycerine further to make it more stable and, therefore, a useful explosive. To do this, he mixed it with silica and made it into rods – dynamite.

Although his discovery made him very rich, Nobel spent many years feeling guilty about his destructive discovery. Over time, laboratory explosions killed his brother Emil and several other people.

Many years later, when Alfred Nobel died, it was discovered that his will contained instructions for his fortune to be used for a series of prizes – Nobel Prizes. These are still awarded today for outstanding discoveries in Physics, Chemistry, Physiology or Medicine, Literature and ironically, Peace.

▼ **Dynamite is highly explosive and produces a lot of smoke.**

7

Making gases

The manufacture of salts is part of the manufacture of hydrogen gas and carbon dioxide gas. When a metal reacts with an acid, not only is a salt produced, but so is hydrogen gas. The equation for this reaction is:

Metal + Acid $\longrightarrow$ Salt + Hydrogen

HYDROGEN GAS

In a school laboratory, you can make hydrogen gas by the reaction between zinc and hydrochloric acid. It is best to use zinc granules because their surface area is large and this increases the rate of reaction.

HOW TO MAKE HYDROGEN

This method of hydrogen collection is called collection over water. It is used for gases that are lighter than air and not very soluble in water.
(1) Place the zinc into a conical flask.
(2) Add hydrochloric acid through a thistle funnel. The acid must fill the thistle funnel.
(3) Next, connect a delivery tube to the flask, fill a trough with water, then place the other end of the delivery tube under the surface of the water.
(4) Cover the delivery tube with a test tube of water.

The reaction that occurs is:

Zinc + Hydrochloric acid $\longrightarrow$ Zinc chloride + Hydrogen

$$Zn_{(s)} + 2HCl_{(aq)} \longrightarrow ZnCl_{2(aq)} + H_{2(g)}$$

The salt remains in the solution. Hydrogen gas travels through the delivery tube into the test tube. As gas fills the test tube, it pushes out the water until eventually bubbles are seen at the surface of the water in the trough. This means that the test tube is full. It is important to insert a bung into the mouth of the test tube whilst it is still under water.

THE TEST FOR HYDROGEN GAS

The test for hydrogen is to insert a lighted splint into the tube. If hydrogen is present, you will hear a loud 'squeaky pop'. The squeaky pop is a mini-explosion. Hydrogen is explosive when mixed with oxygen.

MAKING HYDROGEN GAS

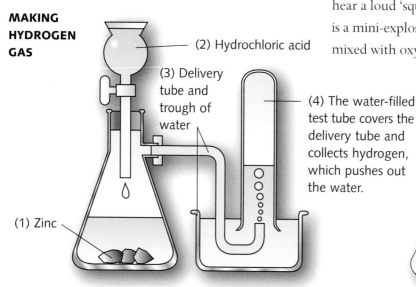

(2) Hydrochloric acid

(3) Delivery tube and trough of water

(4) The water-filled test tube covers the delivery tube and collects hydrogen, which pushes out the water.

(1) Zinc

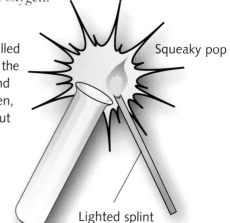

Squeaky pop

Lighted splint

HYDROGEN – USEFUL BUT EXPLOSIVE

Hydrogen is used to make many things from rocket fuel to margarine. Hydrogen is a very light gas. It rises in air, and in the past was used in airships. It is also flammable, and was the cause of a fatal disaster in 1937. During the Hindenburg disaster, approximately one third of the people on board died when an airship dramatically caught

▲ The Hindenburg airship contained hydrogen fuel. It dramatically exploded as it came in to land in New Jersey, USA, in 1937.

fire. There are several theories regarding the cause of the explosion. Some think that a build-up of static electricity ignited the hydrogen, some believe that the airship was sabotaged, and others think that hydrogen leaked from a hole caused by a snapped wire and was ignited by a static electricity spark. Additionally, one school of thought states that it was the covering of the airship (rather than the hydrogen) that provided the fuel.

CARBON DIOXIDE GAS

Carbon dioxide is used in fire extinguishers, fizzy drinks and as stage smoke. If carbon dioxide is cooled down it turns directly into a solid without passing through the liquid stage; this is called **sublimation**. Stage smoke is produced by the sublimation of solid carbon dioxide. Stage smoke is also sometimes called dry ice.

HOW TO MAKE CARBON DIOXIDE

Carbon dioxide is produced by the reaction between an acid and a metal carbonate.

Calcium carbonate + Hydrochloric acid $\longrightarrow$ Calcium chloride + Carbon dioxide + Water
$$CaCO_{3(s)} + 2HCl_{(aq)} \longrightarrow CaCl_{2(aq)} + CO_{2(g)} + H_2O_{(l)}$$

Although there are three products and two reactants, only one of these is a gas – carbon dioxide. The same equipment that is used for hydrogen collection is also used for carbon dioxide collection.

THE TEST FOR CARBON DIOXIDE

When carbon dioxide is bubbled through calcium hydroxide (limewater), it turns it milky. This is because insoluble calcium carbonate forms.

Glossary

ACID – A substance that dissolves in water and releases H^+ ions (protons). Acids have a pH lower than 7.

ACID RAIN – Rain that contains high levels of nitric and/or sulphuric acid and has a pH of approximately 5. Acid rains forms when gases from burning fuels combine with moisture in the atmosphere.

ALKALI – A solution formed by dissolving a base in water. This causes the release of OH^- ions. Alkaline solutions have a pH greater than 7.

BASE – The oxide or hydroxide of a reactive metal, such as sodium. Bases can neutralise an acid and produce a salt. Bases can be soluble or insoluble.

BUFFER SOLUTION – A solution that resists changes in pH when small amounts of acid or alkali are added.

BURETTE – A cylindrical piece of glassware used to measure the volume of a liquid and dispense the liquid from a tap on its bottom end.

CATALYST – A substance that speeds up a chemical reaction without itself being chemically changed.

CORROSIVE – A chemical that destroys metal and/or body tissue.

DISSOLVE – When a solute goes into solution with a solvent.

DOUBLE DECOMPOSITION – A reaction during which two compounds swap chemical partners with each other.

END POINT – The point at which an exact amount of alkali has been added to an acid (or vice versa) for complete neutralisation to have taken place.

EVAPORATE – A physical change from a liquid to a gas.

FILTER – The separation of a solid from a liquid by passing the mixture through filter paper.

HYDRATED SALT – A salt that is bound to water.

ANSWERS

p7 Investigate
(1) The bone will be smaller and pitted because the acid in the vinegar has dissolved the calcium.
(2) The egg should go all the way in. The vinegar has dissolved some of the shell, making it softer.

p11 Investigate
Green/yellow = alkaline.
Red = acidic.

p13 Test yourself
(1) Vinegar – Orange/yellow pH 3
(2) Ammonia solution – Violet pH 11
(3) Pure water – Green pH 7

p22 Test yourself
You would see the formation of an insoluble white precipitate of silver chloride. The two aqueous solutions would form silver chloride and a solution called ammonium nitrate.
$NH_4Cl_{(aq)} + AgNO_{3(aq)} \rightarrow AgCl_{(s)} + NH_4NO_{3(aq)}$

p27 Test yourself
(1) Calcium and sulphuric acid
$Ca_{(s)} + H_2SO_{4(aq)} \rightarrow CaSO_{4(s)} + H_{2(g)}$
(2) Copper and dilute nitric acid
$3Cu_{(s)} + 8HNO_{3(aq)} \rightarrow 3Cu(NO_3)_{2(aq)} + 2NO_{(g)} + 4H_2O_{(l)}$
(3) Magnesium and hydrochloric acid
$Mg_{(s)} + 2HCl_{(aq)} \rightarrow MgCl_{2(aq)} + H_{2(g)}$

p27 Investigate
The iron nail will look corroded. The iron has reacted with the acid and formed a salt. You may also see bubbles of hydrogen gas.

p29 Test yourself
You would mix together magnesium oxide and sulphuric acid. You would then filter the mixture, heat the solution to drive off some of the water and create a saturated solution. You would then leave the sample to crystallise. You would not use the above method to obtain potassium sulphate crystals because potassium oxide (one of the reactants that you would need to use) is soluble.

p31 Test yourself
To make potassium chloride, put a known volume of one of the reactants into a conical flask. Add an indicator to the beaker. Put the other reactant in a burette. Gradually add the reactant from the burette to the flask. When the indicator changes colour, neutralisation has occurred and potassium chloride has formed. Note down the amount of reactant added. Then repeat the process without the indicator so that your final product is not

INDICATOR – A substance that changes colour depending on pH.

INSOLUBLE – A substance that will not dissolve in a given solvent.

ION – An atom that has a charge.

IRRITANT – A substance that causes inflammation on the skin. Irritants usually cause itching when applied to skin.

LITMUS – A type of indicator.

NEUTRALISATION – The reaction of an acid with an alkali that produces a salt and water.

ORGANIC COMPOUND – A compound that contains carbon (except carbon dioxide, carbon monoxide and carbonates). Organic compounds can also contain hydrogen, nitrogen and oxygen.

OXIDISING AGENT – A chemical that easily gives up its oxygen.

PIGMENT – An insoluble coloured substance.

PIPETTE – A piece of glassware used to measure and transfer one volume of liquid.

PRECIPITATE – When a solid separates from solution by chemical or physical change.

SALT – A compound made of positive and negative ions chemically bonded together.

SATURATED SOLUTION – A solution that cannot dissolve any more solute.

STANDARD SOLUTION – A solution of a known and exact concentration.

SUBLIMATION – A physical change from solid to gas or vice versa.

SUSPENSION – A mixture in which fine insoluble particles are dispersed in a liquid.

TITRATION – A chemical method used to determine the concentration of an acidic or alkaline solution.

UNIVERSAL INDICATOR – A mixture of indicators. Universal indicator changes colour across the whole range of pH values.

VOLUMETRIC FLASK – A piece of glassware that accurately measures one volume of solution.

WEIGHING BOAT – A device used to measure the mass of a substance. It comprises a boat-shaped dish that sits on weighing scales. The dish is removable so that it can be easily washed.

coloured. Add the same amount of reactant that you did in the first part of the experiment. Evaporate the solution to a saturated solution over a water bath. Then leave the apparatus in a sunny window for one week. Cover the dish with filter paper to stop dust getting in.

p33 Test yourself
Marble is a metamorphic rock that is made of calcium carbonate. Marble is not porous. This means that it does not contain tiny holes. Therefore it does not allow rainwater to enter and weather the rock. Limestone is a porous form of calcium carbonate. It is easily weathered and eroded by rainwater.

p33 Investigate
There is a fizzing sensation in your mouth caused by the formation of carbon dioxide. The reaction that occurs is:
Citric acid + Sodium hydrogencarbonate ➤
Sodium citrate + Carbon dioxide + Water

Useful websites:
http://www.chem4kids.com
http://www.howstuffworks.com
http://news.bbc.co.uk/1/hi/sci/tech
http://www.newscientist.com

Index

Page references in italics represent pictures.

Photo Credits – *(abbv: r, right, l, left, t, top, m, middle, b, bottom)* **Cover background image** www.istockphoto.com/Mike Bentley **Front cover images** (r) www.istockphoto.com/Joshua Haviv (l) www.istockphoto.com/vera bogaerts **Back cover image** (inset) www.istockphoto.com/vera bogaerts **p.1** (t) www.istockphoto.com/Daniel Slocum (br) Charles D. Winters/Science Photo Library (bl) www.istockphoto.com/oana vinatoru **p.2** Dale C. Spartas/Corbis **p.3** (tr) www.istockphoto.com/Pattie Steib (b) www.istockphoto.com/Iurii Konoval **p.4** (tr) www.istockphoto.com/Ufuk ZIVANA (tl) Charles D. Winters/Science Photo Library **p.5** www.istockphoto.com/Joshua Haviv **p.6** www.istockphoto.com/Jeremy Voisey **p.7** (b) Biophoto Associates/Science Photo Library (t) www.istockphoto.com/Andriy Doriy **p.8** www.istockphoto.com/Anka Kaczmarzyk **p.9** Cordelia Molloy/Science Photo Library **p.10** www.istockphoto.com/Paul Cowan **p.11** (bl) Andrew Lambert Photography/Science Photo Library (tr) www.istockphoto.com/Daniel Slocum (br) www.istockphoto.com/Vera Bogaerts **p.12** Andrew Lambert Photography/Science Photo Library **p.15** Dr Jeremy Burgess/Science Photo Library **p.17** (t) Andrew Lambert Photography/Science Photo Library (b) Andrew Lambert Photography/Science Photo Library **p.20** www.istockphoto.com/Joshua Haviv **p.21** www.istockphoto.com/Weldon Schloneger **p.22** Martyn F. Chillmaid/Science Photo Library **p.23** Sinclair Stammers/Science Photo Library **p.24** www.istockphoto.com/Alan McCredie **p.25** (t) Dale C. Spartas/Corbis (b) www.istockphoto.com/Jeff Griffin **p.26** Charles D. Winters/Science Photo Library **p.27** Charles D. Winters/Science Photo Library **p.30** Richard Megna/Fundamental Photos/Science Photo Library **p.31** Peter Menzel/Science Photo Library **p.32** Martyn F. Chillmaid/Science Photo Library **p.33** www.istockphoto.com/Pattie Steib **p.35** (l) Charles D. Winters/Science Photo Library (r) Burstein Collection/Corbis **p.36** www.istockphoto.com/Anka Kaczmarzyk **p.37** Science Photo Library **p.38** David Taylor/Science Photo Library **p.39** (b) www.istockphoto.com/oana vinatoru (t) www.istockphoto.com/Ufuk ZIVANA **p.40** Mathias Ernert/epa/Corbis **p.41** Dr Jeremy Burgess/Science Photo Library **p.42** James L. Amos/Corbis **p.43** www.istockphoto.com/Iurii Konoval **p.45** Bettmann/Corbis